D0842989

Start TO Finish

Sports Gear

FROM Steel TO Bicycle

ROBIN NELSON

LERNER PUBLICATIONS COMPANY   Minneapolis

Copyright © 2015 by Lerner Publishing Group, Inc.

All rights reserved. International copyright secured. No part of this book may be reproduced, stored in a retrieval system, or transmitted in any form or by any means— electronic, mechanical, photocopying, recording, or otherwise—without the prior written permission of Lerner Publishing Group, Inc., except for the inclusion of brief quotations in an acknowledged review.

Lerner Publications Company
A division of Lerner Publishing Group, Inc.
241 First Avenue North
Minneapolis, MN 55401 USA

For reading levels and more information, look up this title at www.lernerbooks.com.

Library of Congress Cataloging-in-Publication Data

Nelson, Robin, 1971–
    From steel to bicycle / by Robin Nelson.
        pages   cm. — (Start to finish: Sports gear)
    Includes index.
    ISBN 978–1–4677–3892–7 (lib. bdg. : alk. paper)
    ISBN 978–1–4677–4744–8 (eBook)
    1. Bicycles—Design and construction—Juvenile literature. I. Title.
TL410.N45 2014
629.2'3—dc23   2013037397

Manufactured in the United States of America
1 – CG – 7/15/14

TABLE OF Contents

First, steel is heated. — 4

Then steel is shaped into tubes. — 6

The tubes are cut and bent. — 8

Next, a worker welds the tubes together. — 10

After that, the bike is painted. — 12

Workers make the handlebars. — 14

Workers make the wheels. — 16

Next, workers put the bike together. — 18

Finally, the bike is tested. — 20

Glossary — 22

Further Information — 23

Index — 24

I love to ride my bike. How was it made?

First, steel is heated.

Most bike frames are made out of steel. Steel is a metal. A **furnace** heats the steel in a **factory**. The steel gets soft.

Then steel is shaped into tubes.

Machines shape the heated steel into **hollow** tubes.
When the tubes cool, they become strong.

The tubes are cut and bent.

A machine cuts the steel tubes into smaller pieces. Then another machine bends the pieces into different shapes. The tubes fit together like puzzle pieces.

Next, a worker welds the tubes together.

A worker heats the ends of the steel tubes. The ends of the tubes melt together. When they cool, they form strong **joints**. This makes the frame of a bicycle.

After that, the bike is painted.

The bicycle frame is sprayed with paint. Then it is heated until the paint dries. Finally, workers apply stickers with the bike company's name.

Workers make the handlebars.

While the frame is made, workers put together the handlebars. They slide brakes, shifters, and grips onto the bars.

Workers make the wheels.

Machines shape strips of steel into wheels. Workers put in the **spokes**. Then workers test the wheels to make sure they are straight. Rubber tires are added last.

Next, workers put the bike together.

The bicycle frame travels on a **conveyor belt**. As the bike passes by, workers add different parts. They add handlebars, wheels, pedals, and a seat one at a time.

Finally, the bike is tested.

Workers test the bicycle to make sure everything is working. Then the bike is packed up and sent to stores. It's ready to ride!

Glossary

conveyor belt: a moving strip of material that carries things from one place to another

factory: a building where things are made

furnace: a machine that creates heat

hollow: having nothing inside

joints: places where parts are joined

spokes: bars that connect the center of a wheel to the edge

steel: a strong, hard metal

welds: to join metal together with heat

Further Information

Graham, Ian. *The Science of a Bicycle: The Science of Forces.* Pleasantville, NY: Gareth Stevens Publishing, 2009. There's a lot of science behind riding a bike. Learn all about gravity, friction, and more in this book.

Herrington, Lisa M. *Bicycle Safety.* New York: Children's Press, 2012. Check out this book and learn how to stay safe on your bike.

How It's Made: Bicycle Frames
http://science.discovery.com/tv-shows/how-its-made/videos
/how-its-made-bicycle-frames.htm
See how custom carbon fiber bike frames are made in this short video.

Stauffacher, Sue. *Tillie the Terrible Swede: How One Woman, a Sewing Needle, and a Bicycle Changed History.* New York: Alfred A. Knopf, 2011. Read this fun biography of a woman tailor who became a bicycling champion in the 1890s.

Walker, Sally M., and Roseann Feldmann. *Put Wheels and Axles to the Test.* Minneapolis: Lerner Publications, 2012. Did you know your bike is a simple machine? Learn about wheels and axles with fun experiments in this book.

Index

conveyor belt, 18

factory, 4

heating, 4, 10, 12

painting, 12

steel, 4, 6, 8, 10, 16

test, 20

welding, 10
wheels, 16, 18

Photo Acknowledgments
The images in this book are used with the permission
of: © iStockphoto.com/selensergen, p. 1; © iStockphoto.
com/Steve Stone, p. 3; © TDHster/Shutterstock.com, p. 5;
© Sarin Kunthong/Shutterstock.com, p. 7 © Bloomberg/
Getty Images, p. 9, 11; © Ruffer/Caro/Alamy, p. 13;
© Sergio Azenha/Alamy, p. 15; © Uygar Geographic/
Getty Images, p. 17; © Zuma Press/Alamy, p. 19; © Jade/
Blend Images/Getty Images, p. 21.

Front Cover: © iStockphoto.com/balono.

Main body text set in Arta Std Book 20/26.
Typeface provided by International Typeface Corp.